i can
 breathe

i can breathe

carl manlan

Wild Rising Press

EVERGREEN, COLORADO

Published by Wild Rising Press
Copyright ©2025 Carl Manlan

Editor: Judyth Hill
Book Design: Mary M Meade
Book Cover: ARUKA Studio

wildrisingpress.com
ISBN 978-1-957468-45-7

this collection is dedicated to those who
carry the breath of good samaritans who came
before them so they could become.

note / about the cover

aruka studio in lomé, togo designed this cover inspired by the cheetah, an animal whose very body is built around the act of breathing.

the cheetah embodies the central themes of this collection:

breaking free: like a cheetah exploding from stillness to full sprint, these poems move from suffocation to breath, breaking through barriers to find voice and claim space.

solitary strength: cheetahs hunt alone, trusting their own power. these poems trace an individual journey of personal liberation.

vulnerability & resilience: despite their legendary speed, cheetahs are vulnerable to larger predators and must rest, exhausted, after every sprint. this honest acknowledgment of limitations, along with the balance between explosive power and necessary rest, runs through these pages.

grace under pressure: even at maximum speed, the cheetah maintains elegant, focused movement. These poems navigate difficult truths with that same composure.

the abstract design captures the cheetah's essence without literal representation. scattered spots suggest thoughts coalescing into motion, individual breaths forming a larger pattern; beauty in imperfection, identity markers uniquely recognizable. the golden-amber palette evokes warmth, sunlight, earth-grounded hope emerging.

like the cheetah's breathing rate surging from sixty breaths at rest to one hundred fifty during the chase, these poems pulse with the rhythm of survival and transformation.

foreword / before we take a deep breath

if you are reading these words, it is because you are about to open this book *i can breathe*, or are still considering whether to begin. believe me—you should read it. because you are alive. because you love. this is more than a collection of poems; it is an invitation to explore grief as an act of survival, growth, transformation, and shared humanity.

for me, this book carries a special meaning. i had the privilege of witnessing its early stirrings—occasional messages, impromptu conversations between san miguel de allende and buenos aires, glimpses of words becoming something larger. i even read it before it was printed. and, throughout the process, i discovered new and deeper facets of the carl manlan i thought i already knew.

i have known carl for quite some time, since we both worked to advance global health agendas: ending preventable deaths among the most vulnerable and ensuring that people thrive despite hardship. carl, through his roles at the global fund, the un system, african union, ecobank foundation, visa, and other leadership roles. myself, through a uk ngo, the uk parliament, the united nations, and now at caf—the development bank of latin america and the caribbean. in the meantime, we grew older, endured losses, and, i believe, became calmer and perhaps a little wiser.

carl first revealed his passion for writing to a wider audience when he became an aspen new voices fellow. his thoughtful articles on global health and development, particularly on africa, can be found online—and we even co-authored one together. yet, what surprised me most was discovering that his deepest passion for writing lives in poetry.

thus, his first book *i can breathe* is a courageous and beautiful biographical journey told through poems. it carries us through key moments of grief and profound transformation in carl's life. along the way, we meet the remarkable family into which he was born, the family he created with lelani, claire, and liam, as well as mentors, friends, and even strangers whose presence shaped him. these encounters unfold in words and languages gathered from cities, villages, markets, rivers, mountains, and roads stretching from côte d'ivoire to zimbabwe, south africa, ethiopia, the united states, the united arab emirates, mexico, and many other places.

this is also a book about becoming oneself—daring to be different while still carrying the threads of our own personal backgrounds and shared humanity. it moves from the protocol of expressing emotion to the intimate task of defining what it means to be a man on one's own terms.

what i love most about this book is how, in exploring grief, it also opens a window onto carl's own tapestry—and through it, invites us to recognize the "rainbow within" ourselves. we grieve for many reasons: the loss of those who loved us, the loss of innocence when grief was still unknown, the loss of ideas about who we thought we were. carl shows us that grief has power precisely because it is cathartic, unbound by time or space. grieving requires growth.

you can open this book at any page and begin. the poems are companions—reminding us of wisdom we thought we had forgotten, offering perspectives through different lenses. at times they speak of starting small, of taking baby steps. at times of perseverance, stillness, or flexibility. across its four sections—faith in grief, from one to the next, be coming us, and pro spere: according to one's hope—you will encounter poems that take your breath away, steady your breath, or allow you to breathe again. they remind us that if we can grieve, it is because we are alive—quietly, defiantly. and if we can grieve, it is because we are capable of love—patiently, intensely.

in every poem, every verse, every pause, carl encourages us to breathe, to love, to live. and that we must.

susana edjang
monday, 8 september 2025
buenos aires, argentina

preface / i can't breathe

in the beginning, the bible teaches us the lord god formed a
man from the dust of the ground. god breathed into his nostrils
the breath of life; the man became a living being. to live is to
experience grief woven into the rich tapestry of prosperity.
to continue breathing is a promise. broken, at times, by forces
beyond our control. yet it is in lives saved where lie deep roots
of prosperity.

breath taken away by those who did not give it—the anger, the
rage come from these moments. we need to honor the death, the
legacy. now is the time to process the meaning of the gift i had,
to know the man who was my father.

sometimes, we act to preserve without knowing we are enabling
ourselves. a psychologist i saw at the university of cape town
reframed grief for me. "between your father and yourself, there
was nothing left unexplored" before his last breath. she created
a path for grieving. i embraced the choice to be and become. a
rite of passage, for the next generation, in my life.

i remember claire's first breath. i remember liam's first breath.
these are blessed moments. and the blessings become a
responsibility. i became the guardian of their breath. i accepted
the challenge to do all i can to keep them breathing. i did not go
to school to become a father—i had a father who taught me the
importance of saving lives. and in the end, this is what matters,
our own contribution to saving lives.

i was 22 when my father was caught in his own *i can't breathe* moment. he had devoted his life to saving lives. he had chosen to work for others so they might have better health to transform the african continent. a noble cause. interrupted by his murder. no one knows how we will end whether we give the breath of life or not.

i don't know how george floyd's family felt or still feels. each death brings a unique experience. the work to reconcile emotions, hope, and physical presence is complex. one would think it is as simple as breathing. breathing is just a physical activity maintaining life. when one is able to state he cannot breathe, when the audience does not act, our reaction is to seek justice. when the conditions for this act are not addressed, justice is a temporary relief for family and loved ones.

george was not the first one. my father was not the first one. others before them suffered the same fate. many more after them were, are, will be in their *i can't breathe* moment. the outrage for george might be rooted in humanity awakened across the world. covid-19 gave us a shared experience. we were humanized to a certain extent. we were under lockdown and could not just go on with our daily lives. or is it the subliminal impact of a disease attacking the respiratory system? a virus making us aware of our own possible death from virus brutality or from an invisible force.

i can't breathe signals we are at the end of life. we can function with many different body parts broken or at limited capacity. we cannot function without our breath, whatever its quality, so ultimately breath is the decider in ensuring we remain actors in the purpose we have on earth.

i remember my sister's voice, calm and collected, the bearer of the news. our father was no longer breathing. and when breath is gone, when life is gone, it cannot be given again. what matters most is to have known my father and learnt from him, while he was breathing, what it takes to give with purpose.

carl manlan
thursday, 11 september 2025
dubai, united arab emirates
(originally written in cape town in 2020)

contents

ii —   *from one to the next*

iii —   *be coming us*

iv—   *pro spere*

i—faith in grief

in the beginning

when you are born
you are not taught
about grief

maybe
we need not be taught
already in us

at birth is trauma

experience of separation
starting point
beginning
pathway
choice

grief, a companion.

a companion

in the end
a companion
may have a
different path

birth brings grief
                does death take grief away

if death does take grief away
is grief of this world or
the world as we conceive

truth is each generation
accepts grief as a gift left
at the gates of heaven

                to be reduced by each
so each
finds the other grieving less than the previous one

grief
a human companion

1989

coming of age unaware
caught in the midst of being 10
at age 10
life is kind

how did i know
something i did not know
existed so close to me
death was coming

death came like truth
death was already marching on
waiting for the moment
death chose to strike
in solitude
in light

coming from the time
i was born
had nothing to do with me
yet most certainly
everything to do with pépé
how did i know
death was coming

from the time i was born

pépé was present
his embrace warmed me
like love shines in the light
his kiss sealed our bond
a bond broken by death

tears of unknown
sorrow of love
grief of origin

feelings i did not yet know ...

grief hit

grief stayed

tango

life and death
death and joy
joy and grief
grief and peace
peace and love
love and life
intertwine

each tango—
life death and i tangled

in san miguel de allende
unspoken words
found attentive souls

untold stories
found listening souls

our lived life
our coming death
found thirsty souls

our grief united us

writing at last
silence long kept loud inside
finding our shared humanity
now knowing all along we were together

complete strangers
bound by grief
bound by distance
a surprise shock of unity

no one is alone in grief
to tango with grief
is to be whole in transition

grief is passion

siamese

grand remembrance
is an intimate elevation of faith ...

the pain
the separation
the sign of life
the life in tandem

offers the choice to follow another itinerary
towards healing

the journey

grief is a journey in faith
like an artist
sketches the present
stops the past

still we remember
the stamp of approval
the borderless curve
the choice to be together was written
in the seeds of being born again

a seed is rebirth
has to be lived in
to be remodeled
to fit the journey
yet was written

grief reminds us of our humanity
humanity reminds us
we are not alone

god made grief a journey
god distributed grief
equally so unbeknown to us
we could find equality in grief

who would have thought
grief could be a source of prosperity
prosperity is a slow golden sunrise

a gentle touch of light on fields of possibilities
grief is a quiet shadow soft yet deep
a lingering moment of cherished sleep

prosperity is a steady hump of purpose strong and true
a shared horizon planted fresh and sour
a tender echo in the sun and the moon
grief is still a melody of love

at each stop
we get a stamp
we get a border
we get a choice

at each stop
we can be born again

in the name

of the holy mother
of the holy father
on holy day
near the end of 1978
seven days after papa was born
on the day of the immaculate conception
on 8 december 1978
god healed us

pain had a purpose
being born is a miracle
being loved is a blessing
being alive is a miracle

love in distango
sprinkled 4 names on me
kassi from papa's mother
carl from papa's friend
ange from angèle
léopold from papa

ange léopold
became one in moments of doubt
fragile
premature
stained by silent tears
ink of love began to fade

the bearable lightness of being loved

the testimony even doubt ends
a promise whispered in my names
i lived to understand

a choice unmade bears life
a weight in our journey of love

being named means love remained for you
grief simmers in the names

in the names live the weight of grief

remembering

what was your earliest memory
of being alive in love with grief

love was eating *alloco*[1]
grief was unknown

love was playing scrabble
grief was unknown

love was jumping in the rain
grief was unknown

love was in angèle with léopold
grief was unknown

love was constant
grief was making its way

love was holding fragility
grief was silent

love was whispering in the darkest night
grief was ready

love was blooming in the morning grace
grief was hopeful

love was smiling gently
grief knew grief o'clock

grief was contained
love, a companion

grandpa

you were brou kablan marius[2]
pépé was endeared

i remember your smile
the deep lines on your face

i remember your soft voice
the stories whispered of times i did not know

i remember your crisp notes
the importance of saving

i remember your *attièkè-poisson*[3]
love as food

i remember the love for every one of us
the generosity of your soul

i remember your hands
the happiness of my heartbeat

i remember your life
the light you shone
even when you were dimming

i cherish your memory
still see the dancing twinkle in your eyes

silent language
never dies

silence of love

i knew you as a gentle giant
my mother told me
about your time in jail
i heard you did nothing
i heard you accepted fate
i heard how your family survived
i heard how you were never the same
i heard about the sorrow
i heard about the grief
i could not feel grief

how does one feel something running in the blood

i did not feel grief
i did not know how to feel grief
i did not live grief
you did not speak about grief
i did not ask you to name grief

you chose love for us
you chose to let the past be
you were a gentle soul filled with love
your love filled my life

did you know love is the opening act of grief
if you did would you have loved me

love 2.0

when you were in prison
love preserved you
you have always been
love

when waiting for your release
she lived in grief
surrounded by love
with the distance from the prison
reflecting the injustice inside
challenging love bearing grief

we were told you were never
who you were after your release
maybe we accept without understanding
life cannot be the same with or without an injustice

your daughter gave
me love with a caveat—
not to lose me as she lost you

life has different prisons
she overprotected
the fear never left her
her fear of losing you
she loved you as a soul longs

she spoke in tongues
languages of fear with words of love
languages of love with words of fear
sounds of fear with melodies of love
sounds of love with melodies of fear

she was a prisoner of love stolen
never was she in the cell yet lived through
the regret of what it could have been
consumed the energy of what she could be
love had to give

no easy answers

what if love did not exist
where would grief creep in

how does one know love is
what if love was invisible

where would grief creep in
how does one know love is

what if love was a lie
where would grief creep in

how does one know love is
what if love did not exist

grief would not find a way

no easy questions

what if grief did not exist
where would love creep in

how does one know grief is
what if grief was invisible

where would love creep in
how does one know grief is

what if grief was a lie
where would love creep in

how does one know grief is
what if grief did not exist

senses

i was grieving before i knew
i was grieving with my mother while she had me

she had a pregnancy
difficult
i was premature
she was in distress

love with grief
a rite of passage

he was there
by her side

he prayed
he believed
he loved
by our side

he did not let love abandon her
he held on to life he gave her

he believed in the life
breathed in me
he was her papa

he became my pépé

c-section

to come to life
a cut

to breathe to life
a cut

on my first birthday
maman celebrated life
not the cut

on my fifth birthday
maman celebrated hope
not the cut

on my first communion
maman celebrated faith
not the cut

a cut is a scar
a scar is a reminder
a reminder is history
a history is the present lived
in life in hope in faith

geneticode

what if unwritten was coded in the dna
what if grief was written in love
what if love tangles with grief

like in the dna the sequence is written
maktub—it was written
so if it is written we suffer knowing we will overcome

to let them know grief creeped in
we had to go deep into ourselves
to separate weed from roots

the roots from the desert
finding a path in the desert
a path to the oasis following the stars
in our hearts shining in the sky

finding harmony
balancing narrative
so our children act
so each tomorrow
finds them on their
path to prosperity

dna

a lottery
heredity

written before you breathe
love creates heredity
grief scratches the code

code written with love
decoded with grief
love remembers
grief watches

woven with love
deepened with love
wired from roots
separated by grief

love in the desert
grief in the oasis
inevitable destination

falling in love
harmonizing for grief
as the lottery of death is invisible ink
even scratched grief is not decoded

dna is the code unlocked with grief
as heredity is for perpetuity

faith

strong believing in unknown
quiet knowing in you
slow falling in hope

on unseen wings
on unheard tale
on untouched love
on *unsmelled* wounds
on untasted grief

our hopes ascend

sun at midnight

a drumbeat echoes faith in life
a heartbeat pulses faith in birth
the voice beat signals faith in action
the breath beat rhythms faith in passion

passion is the sun at midday

a drumbeat echoes grief in death
a heartbeat pulses grief in still(ness)
the voice beat signals faith in silence
the breath beat rhythms grief in cold

cold is the moon at midnight

grief

what was loved now laid so low

heart pierced ached at the sound of love

whispers of comfort no longer audible

our soul awakened by death echoes from the depth

i am un-strike-able by grief

though tears fell

lights turned down low

spirit dimmed

there is hope in faith

there was forgiveness

forgiveness

whisper i love me

whisper i to your ear
love to your ear
me to your ear

whisper the wind
carry the wind of possibilities
close the gate forgive yourself
for what you could not have known

whisper the melody of your soul

when i did then i forgave
so act with love in you

whisper

to silence

10 years old
pépé in his silence
36 years old
maman in her silence

still on my mind

in the silence
we observe
the hieroglyph
of our entire emotions

still on my mind

imagining in silence
until i enter life after
resolving to be ready
until i consume my past
passing on understanding
until grief comes

she knew
she silenced
she protected

us

who protected us
when her time came
why did we lose all

god knew

silence

we mourn

still on my mind

like the hieroglyph
of my future
written in signs
harmony the decoder

at the time
i did not know
silence

death coming

surprise in the night
of the echo
of the last breath

heard inaudible by the senses
pulsated at the rhythm of the last beat
the melody passed on
isn't a gift for us only

but for the next generation
though they need not carry
the part the parents had to deal with

each generation must resolve
her part of the heritage
in grief

she knew
she did not say
maybe she hoped it would not be
how do you know
if life is over at the last breath

if it is then why do we sense
presence and absence

grief visits us
like a thief in a broad day light
like a thief in dark night light
like a thief in the warmth of our illusions of eternity

it was written

reminder

on the 3rd day
death reminded love
jesus

to carry a cross
on the final day
death came down the cross
jesus

death is love
death comes knocking
when

doubt makes death matter

death is certain
no matter how the night is
death like day
is sure to come

become sad

i encountered sadness
on my way to pépé

maman carried the cross
on her own

the nurse who knew
the nurse who believed
the nurse who breathed life
the nurse who tried

the daughter who could not
the sister who could not
the niece who could not
the mother who could not

death is love
jesus died on the cross
the cross we let go

maman i did not know
pépé was no longer

maman experienced something

all i could feel did not match
anything i knew as words did not match
numb maybe
sadness is the word for that moment

simply my first experience of grief

april 1989

first communion
first burial

on this holy day
god gave us

death and faith
given and taken in harmony

death the promise
faith the step in between

on this holy day
god gave us

death is eternity
death is instant
death is transition

on this holy day
god gave us

faith opens gift
faith creates communion
faith numbs pain

on this holy day
god gave us

death challenged faith
pépé was
faith called death

pépé was no longer
death ignited faith
pépé was rested
faith whispered death
pépé is my angel

on this holy day
god gave us

ii—from one to the next

ode to joy

on this holy day
god gave us

papa
you stood by me

papa
you celebrated with me

papa
you did what a papa does

showed me the light
kept the light on

in this dark hour

never evoked the past
never called on the past
never reminded me

stood in the silence
of your faith

read faith in your eyes
made love visible
as pépé laid to rest in aboisso⁺

el maestro

you gifted us love
you believed in words
you sprinkled acts of love

like spices on raw meat
you knew love was an act
you gave flavors to love

you gifted us love
you believed in words
you sprinkled acts of love

like spikes in shoes
you knew spikes needed traction
you gave meaning to movement

56

you gifted us love
you believed in words
you sprinkled acts of love

like tiny pulses within brain
you made connections
you gave meaning to heart

you were love
you were movement
you were heart

integrity

a quiet strength
a steady hand
a gift of truth

you acted in harmony
you showed compassion
you spoke anger
you nudged in peace

i cheated

you raised your voice in disgust
you raised your decibels in shock
you raised your hand with force

i reacted

my flesh raised
my mind cleared
my commitment to integrity
sealed under my skin

i learned

so you never had

and i never

your silence respected my pain

your silence
hung as love in the air

i breathed relief
i caught integrity

i vowed

i never

pace of life lessons

whisper heard
urgent candor
in the early hours
when even the dew
had not yet kissed the sun

your gentle firm voice
often broke my dreams
time did not matter
as silence of dew wetted our feet
before rays shone on us

your pace
rhythm of fresh words of the morning
sparkling with the wisdom they carry
wisdom carried into an unsettled mind
intergenerational life lessons

your breathing
slow and steady
me, absorbing words
me, connecting dots
me, *perdu* life lessons

you taught me
how to love walking
you created a beautiful place
for you to be with me
we stood side by side

not knowing yet
one day we will no longer walk

i did not know then
you told me before it happened

the ending came
in the afternoon of my youth
while they took you out
in the night when your shadow
could no longer protect you

we no longer walk together

i walk alone
still remembering you
still standing by your side
knowing walking was a gift
of your eternal love

60   we no longer walk

i told claire
i told liam
they are not ready to walk
we each have our own love language
this was ours
need not be theirs

i never walk alone

whisper of death

brazzaville sent you home
as gun fires of 1997 silenced lives

harare[5] called you
you answered with us in mind
us together

reimagining who
we are at an altitude of 1483 meters
how we elevate
at higher altitude
the walking tradition

before i understood our plan
you had me
at your very distinct
way of crafting
how love matters

come away with me
norah jones took
a cue from you

you did not write me a song
you laid the foundation
inner peace
so misfortunes and belongings in me
will always be a part of the why

so i know
when time came
you did with heart
no lies to cloud our path

cloud may form with absence
dissipate under the weight of love
love instilled grows without doubt
is carried through memory
injustice creeped in waiting for hitmen
i could see the path as love is

come away with me
waking up before the dew kisses sun
safe in my arms
you taught me eternal love

you left loving
even in the pain suffered

whispers loud
last murmur of agony

our tomorrows in the night
shine with the light
of your heart

until

up until the point
where no longer possible
we learnt about the journey
we designed what we could
we created the peace
we said made sense

we spoke the first time
as if sentences were a continuation
an extension of conversations
started in the streets of riviéra
our friend believed
before we understood

we took the steps knowing
a pause was coming
we did not know what could be
we knew our flights will end
the beauty
the simplicity
at dawn before the light came

life itself is a transition
awakens us to possibilities
we did not know
need not know
to live fully in the time given

we did

january 1998

air afrique
pan-african symbol
along fields of the ébrié lagoon
a young heart took his flight
took a deep breath
imagined the map
abidjan was clear in the night
heads in the clouds
in the distance foggy johannesburg
blurred harare

air afrique
pan-african symbol
took my last breath in abidjan
tears rolled on the promise of the unknown
bidding adieu to a land i germinated
fear of the unknown to a land where seeds are sown

how could i imagine

air afrique
pan-african symbol
delayed in an unfamiliar space
where emotions cloud aspirations
by the window the runway stretched
buried in heavy wet thoughts
of feelings under the moonlight
not knowing in a silent prayer
what tomorrow might bring
chasing a long-held dream
engines roared as the world began to sing
the silent melody of transformation

below the familiar tapestry of a whole life
above the future i could not imagine
far from my childhood town

air afrique
pan-african symbol
took my first breath in johannesburg
eyes narrow red
greetings in 11 languages
sawubona[6]
crossed emotional boundaries
a language new to learn
this journey to another land
a path of possible return
how could i imagine

south african airways
my passport created confusion
never seen but insisted visa required
long discussion born from ignorance
africa's achilles' heels
my first breath in harare
raw above the sea level
a new self a whispered invisible wraith

toyota
rode to town numbed by new feelings
conflict between optimism of the unknown
leap of faith letting faith reveal itself
eyes wide open
mind in abidjan
heart in trauma
soul put to test
rolling with the jacarandas
the avenues as a soft landing

how could i imagine

harare where shona[7] and agni[8] meet
could i imagine harare
a place younger than me
could i imagine harare
a place of stone culture
i could yet when
history under western influence
geography under western influence
foundations shifted
going south opened eyes, mind, heart, soul to the road less
    traveled

i could imagine

immigrant

harare
gave me everything i needed
speciss college for shamwari
english a world dialect
english a gate opener

harare
gave me everything i needed
seeds for adulthood i picked
papa my compass
papa my partner

harare
gave me everything i needed
a friend for life
sister cristina my faith mentor
sister cristina my learning partner

harare
gave me everything i needed
path forward
pieces of african identity
premise of an african education
a white envelope to university of cape town

harare
gave me everything i needed
a father i longed to know
me i longed to know
fatherhood compost

harare
gave me everything i needed

watched over us
got to know about your etymology
he who does not sleep never sleeps
the chief nickname
loaned to name you
shona language
evoked peace

why didn't you whisper
maybe you did in shona
a voice in shona
an ear in agni
lost in translation

death was in motion

family's echo

what is family
when distance is a test

what is a test
when emotion is venom

what is venom
when bite is a kiss

what is a kiss
when joy is a curse

what is a curse
when the river dies

hope is a mirage
when the baobab
stands testament to resilience

what is resilience
when the drumbeat fades
laughter is memory

what is a memory
when ancestors
whisper in twilight

what is a curse
when distance
is a stranger

what is a stranger
when the sunrise

paints the sky

one we ought to accept
as dawn brings new beginnings
in your own family

solo dialogue

he planned
he planted
he knew

together
a beautiful
place to be

i followed
i germinated
i learnt english

together
a beautiful
place to be

he observed
he listened
he knew

together
a beautiful
place to be

i discovered
i nurtured
i applied

together
a beautiful
place to be

he guided
he molded
he knew

together
a beautiful
place to be

i waited
i received
i left

together
a beautiful
place to be

how did i not hear
the whisper of the soul

shamwari[9]

you appeared with
grace sympathy authenticity

you invited
faith peace courage

you showed
humanity experience service

i shared
empathy curiosity vulnerability

i learned
ardere et lucere[10]
inner fire
knowledge for service
faith for service

i echoed
grace simplicity authenticity

we believed
doubt whispered
doubters screamed
doubters believed

faith
living testimony
pure

avenues to lincoln green

avenues in harare
lined with jacarandas
lincoln green
indian neighborhood

avenues
length you evoke
first steps in unknown
the peace

lincoln green in harare
defined by the majority
exist as one of the few
identity by opposition
war in my head

avenues
soft landing

lincoln green
transition to race

avenues
sheltered by trees
protected by familiar
assurance by habit

lincoln green
exposed by race
exposed by accent
exposed by curiosity
of an immigrant

i walk your streets
africans as gardeners
blacks as house help
i same race
yet different
race is a creation
until you are
defined by

mother city[11]

early on you embraced me
before i met you
you embraced me
like a mother does

later on you covered me
after i looked at you
you layered me
with clouds on table mountain

i was not alone
even when you did not clear the clouds
for me to see death

you are a mother
mothers protect
even when time
to leave the nest
to face the world
not always smiling at us
a path to inner peace is in whispering
what you knew
before death emerged

yet i *tatenda*[12] you

everything

cape town
you gave me everything i did not know
a university degree
an african heritage
a vision for africa
seeds

cape town
you gave me everything i did not know
failing as a path to meet a wife
learning about english nuances in multiple choice questions
freedom to become at my pace
faith to believe in good samaritans

cape town
you gave me everything i did not know
saying goodbye even when tomorrow never came
believing in farewell when the end was nigh
feeling a last hug
keeping the memory of what it was
the image of the last wave

cape town
you gave me everything i did not know
why didn't you whisper death was in motion

drip

when did he know
it was the last touch
it was the last time
it was the last trip

he said goodbye
not understanding
he knew

when did papa know
it was the last ride
it was the last drive
it was the last stop for us

he said goodbye
not feeling
he knew

when did papa know
it was their plan
it was their will
it was their power

he said goodbye
i froze understanding
he knew

may
maybe
maybe not the last time
maybe not the last handshake
maybe not the last embrace
maybe not the last look in the eyes

what would have dripped
if i understood the end

nothing
pre-emotion does no justice
trigger required
bullet piercing
impact boum
siren of the soul

the beginning

leaking news

when do you know
it is the last time
he came to say goodbye

he knew

when the driver came
he did not want me
to go with him

he knew

when the car drove
he waved

he knew

in his mind
he trusted
a friend
betrayed

he knew

in may
i saw him one last time
i held his hand one last time
i read love in his eyes
it was the last hug

what would have i done

if i had understood what he said

seeds

first week of november
illness visited me
weak without borders

you called on a sunday
the day god has given us
to rest

you called on a holy day
the day god has given you
to seed

you called
on a weak day
the day god has given us
to fertilize

you called
on a family day
the day god has given you
to water the seeds

you called
one last time
so you will not leave unannounced

i did not understand

04 11 2001

on a given sunday
one takes word
as it comes

in the light
when light is dimming
yet shines brightly

distance gave
technology power
for the last walk

you felt
me not knowing
our last walk
was virtual
you whispered
in the midst
last breath

you knew
you spoke family
you asked care
you sighed peace
in the midst
violence
last breath

you planted the bullet
for the imminent grief trigger
you did what you could
without asking me to understand
i did not

i did not know
it was the last walk
you would not wake me up again

you said one last time
love

i did not know
it was the last walk

20 11 2001

on this holy day
god has given us
henri-michel
lelani
i

century city mall
flight to abidjan
travel agent did not know
where abidjan was
we left bemused

his soul signaled mine
going to abidjan was written in grief letters
the trigger waited

you had planned our coming together
a first christmas in many years
with all us at home together

nokia 3310 rang
daddy not seen at office
voice at the limit of acceptance
calm yet fragile
soft yet aggravated

by the time
3310 rang again
i was in rondebosch
henri-michel
lelani
i

a fisherman found the body
grief triggered
kandahar on cnn
different murder scenes
shared experience of grief

world span
heart beat to love lost
eyes rinsed my soul
i breathed
not my last
papa had taken
his last breath

going home

is death true
he who does not sleep
awakens in the grief
of remembrance

harare
you gave me everything i needed
you called me home
you never told me
whether you knew

harare
you gave me a papa i know
he called so i could know him
i responded so i could know me
now he would no longer be
he had said goodbye to you
did you know

when he left us in may
we would mourn together in november

harare
you taught me
what he meant by
love is action
i saw through years
commitment to better health for all
did you know health kills
when money enters
unstable minds

harare
even if you knew
why whisper *bujumbura*

harare
even if you knew
why whisper *lake tanganyika*

lake tanganyika
whispered death
fisherman heard
whispered body
world heard

harare
you gave me everything i needed
tatenda
thank you
merci
dankie
mi da wa se
murakoze

home

abidjan
whisked in the middle of the night
under the night stars
i counted to confirm
only one star was missing

i looked eyes closed
at the last memory of our time in abidjan
it was december 1997 our month
you had these tender words:
viens avec moi à *harare. si tu ne viens pas on aura pas l'occasion de se
     connaître.*[13]
i longed for knowing you
you knew
did you know harare was the last
place for us

you gave us 25 years
karen was 25 years 3 months
she heard death whisper
you set the timeline
you respected your word
we were on our own
i had 3 more years
where do i claim them

how could one grieve when
all was already said
is it fair to you
or was it the murder they wrote
you were dead
force of nature or human complicity

irrelevant
your last breath was taken away

you breathed in us as you promised
values your mother taught you
so when time came
we knew she has been
waiting for you

so how can we hold you
when the one who breathed in you
has been waiting for you
we are grateful for your most
precious gift
time

as humans we created rituals
to honor our egos
so we did what we could under
the weight of tradition

in abidjan
in aboisso
in ayebo[14]
to cry is not *akan*
a man does not cry
a man makes his emotions go
a man stands in the well of his emotions
a man suppresses for the blood runs deep
a man honors the dead in the dignity of silence
a man looks for peace in the sudden death of his emotions

a man is still alive with emotions

in cape town
in the silence of my head
i cried tears of joy
your life was a gift
no matter how ended
you gave me everything
you gave us everything
you gave you fully

ayebo

flesh bids farewell
soul watches silence
last ritual for closure

what is closure
when one can
neither touch nor feel grief
foreign death birthed a hole
brutality led murder
ending in the land of the ancestors

on this holy day god has given us
burial on birthday
giving and taking away
a repeat of the first communion
1989 blueprint for 2001

life intertwined with death
renaissance in faith

tears

uphold masculinity in silence
uphold strength in silence
uphold tradition in adversity

tears weaken
the fabric of society
in public masculine identity

heroic gesture
of weak internal strength
pillars of strength in families
communities around and beyond

emotions cried out
cloud judgement
like the soul calls for relief
tears pressure breaker
of excess
yet a sign of inability

in quiet silent soul
regenerative

in the midst of the funeral
i found an escape
rinsed my soul
i was caught behaving against
principles of masculinity

remaining time
held my tears
in my soul's bladder

waiting for the solo flight to cape town
to drown in sorrow

uphold masculinity in adversity
uphold strength in weakness
uphold tradition on earth

iii—be coming us

volcano

we stood on the edge of love

we did not have to
we chose peace

we accepted differences
life brought us
i could no longer be
the one you let go in 1998

i was no longer
you barely accepted your education
required distance to mature me

i looked at the work i smiled
i did not tell you enough
how much i am who
because you did
who i am

i am only beginning
to be who you created
even in the ignorance
of what harare cape town
contributed to the foundation

a volcano has quiet strength
a mountain deep with sleeping secrets
with distant pathways cracked
you let lava flow
fiery grace
clearing the ground

for our new space
sealing the cracks
letting ash make life
starts anew
you taught me love
a force forever true

unconditional

love expressed
love received
you wished for a better life
you chose to live life through us

a sacrifice

patience expressed
patience received
you wished for unity
you chose
to live life with us

a sacrifice

me coming to life was one
yet you celebrated a blessing
yet when time came
to fly you kept the wings
hidden as fear gripped
yet you knew love
has to let fly
for destiny to knock faith into my path
destiny without faith became conditional love
yet you wanted better in the dawn of your thoughts
yet in the midday of your thoughts you could not feel light
    without me

a sacrifice

so in the twilight of your night
you set me free

morning came as wings stretched
for the flight of a lifetime

a sacrifice

for words unspoken of dreams abandoned
at the birth of your children so each could live
dreams dreamt before they caught their first breath

you sacrificed unconditionally
for light to shine in us even
when yours dimmed slowly

a sacrifice called love

gratitude

you said you did life for us—i saw
your life was a sacrifice—i felt

you had wanted to continue your studies
pépé in jail brought limited resources

you became hungry for success
living your dream through us

i vowed

you said you did life for me—i knew
your life was a sacrifice
i offer gratitude to you
i danced to tune
into your love

your life was a sacrifice—i felt

you said you did life for me
i said i am grateful
my life is all because of you
i said i am

i am unresolved

bonding

one of our moments
the market in treichville
the silent admiration of a son

the dialects you spoke fluently
your ability to negotiate
in grace sparkled humility

i watched you in admiration
i picked up the words
i harnessed the skills

the words
commanding respect
in reciprocity
the reciprocity
improving skills

the skills
acknowledging
power of the seller
the seller
remembering
your preferences

the preferences
creating
a bond
the bond
reflecting
human connection

to this day
i cherish
our memory
my memory
learning
by observing you

i did not have the skills
i did not have the words
you knew
by being by you
i would learn
i would remember
i would carry forward

to this day
i cherish
our memory
my memory
being by your side
i did not always have patience
i did not always have understanding
i did not always have gratitude

i understand now
i can no longer express love
i can only pray for forgiveness
to this day
i cherish
our memory

differently

what if i loved you differently
we missed the transition
independence rhymed with rejection

i trusted through space
you trusted through box

i was no longer
the child you raised
the adult you never saw
coming to maturity

who am i to dispute
your wisdom built in hardship

yet a mind
you raised to be independent
even of you

with love
with growth

i am unresolved

baking

you baked to teach me
about work
about money

you baked to teach me
about life stages
about rising
about falling

by your side
to measure
the right flour
to break the right eggs
to add the right oil

the steps under the heat
taught me belonging
patience observation

you loved baking
to whisk agility
speed with conviction
consistency with taste
as love was the glue

you knew
how to take over
you would read
the loss of strength
gently taking over
so i could watch you whisk

i admired the strength of your arms
i saw the change in the consistency
i smelled the mixture
i tasted from the spoon
under your tender eyes

you loved baking

we bonded
we knew
we smiled
we cherished the present
unknowing the end of eternity

the rainbow within us

there is no age to admire a rainbow
i don't remember the last time
we saw one together
i longed for them to be closer
to see the overlap between the hues

we lost our yellow in the night
we could not see the missing hue in the night
in the morning his sun did not light
the space in between widened
we did not close the gap

we knew there was a gap
buried aspiration to close
unable to reconcile suddenness with our own hues
to create a new shade of yellow
even a dimmed one
yellow lightens the heart
broken hearts see no light

yet we remembered yellow
bright like the midday sun
dimmed like the sunset
low dark light like dusk
there was still life
life at darkest hour

hope came in the early hours
when orange signaled light
not as bright as before
every day brings his tomorrow
for peace to be upon us

peace regenerates the fertile soil of the soul
in the baby blue of hope

if hope was *maktub*
we have to sprinkle violet
the passage of bravery and independence
to indigo the mosaic of our lives

life is in us

honoring the memory

melody of the future
notes of the present
whispers of the past
wishes at birth may not come to pass
they are sprinkled on the imaginary path
until the first baby step creates a pathway

baby steps are wobbly
it gets better yet the line is not straight
the path was filled with stories of lives saved
the sketch of the future was drawn with women in the markets
the purpose was human
yet success had a definition
banker

crossed the starting line
after you departed
the melody of the future
the notes of the present
the whispers of the past
written in a language
i could bear

accra and lomé
homes of the pan-african banking dream
opened their back doors to the dream
you echoed so a son could
step into the destiny you crafted

if i had told you
i was an artist
you would have laughed silently

while nudging me
to be who you believed
i could become

if i had told you
i could be both
you would laugh silently
while nudging me
to fulfill the promise
in my name

yet melody of the future
did not sing the harmony
of my soul
the notes of the present
did not tune to finance
the whispers of the past
sang saving lives

in politics
in philosophy
in economics
i found a path
you were proud
on graduation day

i was proud to have
made you proud
yet in failure
i saw my light
yet in failure
i met prosperity
yet in failure
i met good samaritans

a son's duty to honor
honor mother
banker through back door
on the eve of your death
in days following your burial
ecobank confirmed

i entered the gates of your heaven
as you rested

iv—*pro spere*

according to one's hope

lanipani[15]

on the footsteps
of table mountain
we took our first step

what started as a silent conversation
about where i departed from
to land on the shores of cape town
became a puzzle

our storytelling revealed meaning
cultural differences neither seen nor heard
weaved into the simple joy of being

in being
we knew we were crossing
racial lines in existence
long before we were born

even though
1994[16] claimed the past
we were still in the midst
of the most painful transition
the mind had to adapt to the reality
fear is the first step
once taken love takes over

because fear
even rooted in color is temporary
running in invisible veins is the same color

so we went about walking
from the steps on campus to the world of the northern
    suburbs

as we prepared to embrace the world of differences
our ticket to the future was written in african

what is a ticket to the future
when companionship is missing
so we agreed under the loving
eye of my sister to hold hands
on this journey called love
at patient sight

we did not know how life would
bring imagination to the union
love is work
hard work
when destiny is *maktub*
love is to be accomplished
searching for the missing pieces

of the puzzle becomes a lifelong commitment

we did not hold all of them yet
time came to search for meaning in geneva
you were mature and ahead of my emotional intelligence
when i said i cannot
you left with bags of sorrow i did not carry
i searched for the missing pieces in my soul

as time lifted the veil
i understood the missing piece
was my own journey to understand
why

in the silence of my soul
i found the path
prepared to cross the river of my fears

to meet you on the shores
of the happiness you held inside

even as time escaped us
there was beauty in the fire
ignited in faith

learning papa

to love is to act
to act is to seek
to seek is to find
to find is to discover
to discover is to learn
to learn is to have patience

patience is love

you listened to me
i believed you understood
i did not speak *gaga gigi gougou*
i spoke french as agni dissipated
i listened to your sounds
i imagined our conversation
a monologue in words in smiles and senses
yet a conversation in sound with soul
i waited for your first words

patience is love

i listened to you
you believed i understood
you did not speak *gaga gigi gougou*
you created sounds
you smiled
you believed i understood
you raised your silent voice
as signals of discomfort
you expressed with your eyes
our imaginations made our conversation
i learnt to understand your silent language

patience is love

you grew in harmony
your light shining on you
every day you gave us love
love we did not know
every day you gifted us life
three to tango

every day your light shone on us
light as clear as your name
claire

every day you gave us
light
love
to be guardians of your breath
to help destiny meet you
dawn of your life

patience is love

love is light
light is presence
presence is constant
constant is heartbeat
heartbeat is life
life is gift
gift is god
god is god

baobab

grief is a seed
prosperity is a baobab
a woman standing strong and free

standing on the shores of côte d'ivoire
i remember the sweetness of the pineapple
the bitterness of the student life
i remember the rich cocoa farms
blossoming with the labor of love
rooted in the bitterness of cocoa prices
the sweetness of the transformation
a promise rooted in the past
sorrow woven in the fabric of old despair
scent of growth beyond compare is approaching

standing on the shores of south africa
i remember the sweetness of the watermelon
the bitterness of the student life
i remember the rich vineyards
blossoming with the labor of love
rooted in the bitterness of history
the sweetness of the transformation
a promise rooted in the past
sorrow woven in the fabric of old despair
scent of rainbow beyond compare is approaching

standing on the ethiopian highlands
i remember the sweetness of the history
the bitterness of a whispered cloud
echoing the drought that scarred the world
i remember the rivers where new life was fed
blossoming with the boldness of vibrant fabrics

rooted in the bitterness of coffee
the sweetness of the aroma
as history reminds us seeds of hardship
root belonging sprout new hopes

standing on the shores of togo
i remember the sweetness of the *nana benz*[17]
the bitterness of a generation who failed their mothers
i remember the beating heart of trade in west africa
where trade routes winding through
villages eased pain through the divine work
only women can be trusted with
rooted in the bitterness of grief
the sweetness of struggles etched in lines so deep
for children to keep the promise of a grand design
beyond compare imagined by the *nana benz*

grief

the seed buried deep within
stands at the root of the baobab
where new hopes begin
prosperity a woman
a grace

31.13

dieu t'a choisi pour être reine
reine remplie de bonté
bonté divine qui est en toi
toi née ce 31 mai 2012

avec ta lumière claire
claire tu es lumière
ta lumière illumine
nos vies

vies qui sont devenues brillantes
brillantes par ton arrivée

en ce jour béni que
dieu nous donne

je te souhaite
une vie pleine
une vie bénie
une vie éclairée

31.13

you were born to reign
queen of heart overflowing
overflowing with light not your own
late spring daughter

brilliance streams from you
streams you are the source
your presence ignites
our days

days turned golden
golden the moment you arrived

on this gift of a morning
the universe gave

I dreamt for you
fullness upon fullness
blessing upon blessing
fire upon fire

02 09 11

a quiet charm
a steady hand
a wise soul
you walk through life in gentle ways

eleven years
a thoughtful height
you see beyond the fading light
on solid quiet ground
you're found

you stand apart
a gentle david
absorbing melodies of life
unspoken thoughts
undiscovered fears
you hold them all within your years

a heart that knows the tender art
you read the room with calm
grace your presence with space

stand tall
you know your worth
quiet strength gift of earth
you're built to shine
a patient sun.

primavera

at the *primavera* of your prosperity
would you be an alaskan wood frog
in spring

in the *invierno* of your doubt
prosperity awaits
frozen nights
miracle slow
yet no warmth
deep instinct
the promise
stillness in heart
no pulse
fragile
yet deep belief
grief hardens
yet miracle deep
within awaits primavera

in *otoño*
whispers crisp
whispers cool
abiding by nature's rule
beneath leaves sheltered strength
gathered for the slumber
not hoarding gold
lasting riches for harsh unseen
planned with care keenly
wisely
as prosperity puts on warm boots
in the silence of the snow
departed yet still

in *verano*
wisdom held
gene preserved
wood frog thrives
energy from primavera
master of vibrancy
dining wild
digesting free
embracing life
sprung from eggs in the grand future
as new generations bless the land
creating forests in the twilight
while basking in the midday sun
in the afternoon of their desire
to prosper for future
as present unfolds
sunny
rainy
growing green with lush
harvesting prosperity
widely shared

in primavera
frost still bites
frozen nights
miracle slow
growing heart
instinct deep
deep secrets
of woven dna
prosperity protected
frosted jewel
beneath the sun
loud chorus of life
crowd of whisperers

telling fortunes of survival
of artistic testament
of god's creation
reminding us
even when heart stops breath stops
shining through summer solstice

at the primavera
of your prosperity
be you

dawn

at the dawn
of your life
as grief creeps in
what would you
remember

a life filled
with prosperity

a life filled
with grief

in the beginning
breath is given
for prosperity
with a caveat

in the beginning
one does not know
what family
what geography
means

as life progresses
prosperity arrives
every morning

like dawn
grief arrives
every morning
in the twilight
of doubt

yet strength
is being human

in saving lives
my parents turned
a profession
into streams of blessings
for generations to come

three years
after papa's murder
the gentleman from peru opened
the gates of geneva

my dawn
my doubt
my prosperity

transmission

être vieux
assis sur
le bout de bois de dieu
je vois plus loin que claire et liam

claire et liam
assis sur la branche
prôche de la cime
de leur jeunesse
croient en ce que leurs yeux voient

de ce dilemme
naît la joie d'être soi
de conjuguer au présent
le passé qui fait afin que le futur
soit un temps présent
pour absorber les elements de la mission donnée

je suis le serviteur
de la mission que dieu
vous a confié

passing it on

to be elder
seated on heaven's old timber
i see beyond where claire and liam see

claire and liam
perched on branches
close to the canopy
of their becoming
trust what their eyes can hold

from this gap
blooms the gift of selfhood
of making the past
present tense
so the future turns
into now
receiving what the calling asks

i serve
the work heaven
placed in your hands

time

take the time
you are given
to simply
to *complexly*
be you

being you
is a unique
value creation
to the world
embracing you

though you may
not see
you are patiently
germinating you

take the time
you are given
to simply
to *complexly*
be you

being you
is a solo experience
to the world

though you may
not feel
you are preparing
for the moment

take the time
you are given
to simply
to *complexly*
be you

being you
is wealth
to the community

though you may
not count
you are accumulating
compound interest

take the time
you are given
to give to *autrui*

silence

in the early hours
when moon lingers

i think of night lingering
as if to remind silently
even in the lightest hour
night is present

silence obscuring gentle fire
still going about to die
yet can be revived

be the light
shining in your
darkest hour

golden

falling

as you open your eyes
dreams dreamt
bring emotions

as you close your eyes
dreams abandoned
bring emotions

as you open your eyes
words fall into reason

what if

brings
silent words
unspoken
unfound-able

what if

creates
spare words
spoken known
found fallen into
the creativity
sparked by
your dreams

brother & sisters

born in a group
you did not choose

trained to
love one another

choose to continue
or not

whatever the path
your presence
was part of
prosperity

it was in unsaid
it was in silence
it was in emotions

as you look back
hold on to parts made you

no matter how you feel
today is
because us

be you

to be seen
to be heard
to be touched
to be smelled
to be spoken

be you
with what you get

blossom
with what you have

idea

i am your idea
what would
you do with me

what temperature
works for you
some like
hot idea

do they know
if right temperature

what temperature
works for you
some like
cold idea

do they know
if money prefers hot

what temperature
works for you
some like
warm idea

do they know
if investors like warm

whatever temperature
make your idea work for you

peso

i do not have
to carry the peso
of tomorrow

you have to be with me
in the moment of our today

i do not have to lift
the burden of tomorrow

you have to be with us
in the past of our today

i go with you together
knowing tomorrow never comes

as tomorrow is a place
where only today matters

hide

i seek you because you hid

you hid because
you knew i'd look for you

would you hide
if i would not seek you

such is prosperity

trust

you can breathe

when you reach the end
you can breathe

breathe

you just began

breathe

when you begin
you create

breathe

breath begins at the trauma of life

breathe

life continues with trauma

breathe

today begins with trauma in mind

breathe

tomorrow ends farther than today

breathe

trauma in the past
life in the now
all more to come

breathe

you are breathing
you are becoming

endnotes

[1] fried plantain

[2] grandfather's name

[3] cassava semolina with fried fish

[4] a city located in the sud-comoé region of southeastern côte d'ivoire

[5] capital of zimbabwe

[6] a zulu greeting honoring the person you are

[7] bantu ethnic group

[8] a branch of the akan ethnic group

[9] friend in shona

[10] to burn and to shine

[11] cape town

[12] thank you in shona

[13] come with me so we get to know each other

[14] village near aboisso

[15] childhood nickname

[16] year of south africa's first democratic election

[17] a group of influential and wealthy togolese women who built fortunes trading Dutch wax-print (batik) fabrics, and who were nicknamed for the mercedes benz cars they drove

afterward / after we took a deep breath

for carl, for all who grieve love

these words do not conclude the story of these poems. they are an opening—a reminder that even when grief narrows the world, breath can widen it again. what's lost does not vanish; it transforms. it lives on.

for me, *i can breathe* is a meditation on presence—how we are given it, how we hold it, how we lose it, and how it continues, often in unexpected forms. i paint to hold on to that presence. carl writes so it won't disappear. his poems move like memory through flickers of light and shadow—fragile, resonant, alive.

i now know what it means—as maya angelou wrote—to feel, when great trees fall, and "even elephants lumber after safety," the world shift. there is the great ripple of a presence lost, and quieter ripples that continue to shape those left behind.

carl's father lives here, not as memory, but as presence. "father taught me the importance of saving lives," he writes, "and what it takes to give with purpose." that legacy echoes. claire and liam inherit those echoes. i feel it too—in my mother, whose life began in a small scandinavian village and was transformed by the ingenuity, injustice, humanity, passion, and humor she encountered during her years in lagos. she passed on an unshakable belief in dignity and humanity—and carried that gently, but fiercely, to her last breath.

it's said that death is the great equalizer. but as carl reminds us, "each death brings a unique experience." grief is not one thing. it's as personal as a breath, as singular as a name. i was there when my mother died. i held her hand. i heard her final breath. carl could not. his father was taken suddenly, violently. both losses, but they shape the heart differently. still, what connects us is what the poems reveal: if we can grieve, we are—thankfully—capable of love.

grief, i've come to believe, is love without a home.
but in these poems, carl builds one.
a space where we don't have to resolve sorrow—just carry it.
recognize it. let it breathe.

this book doesn't try to fix grief—it honors it. and i am thankful for that. absence is not only loss. it is also space—where something might return. a spark, a memory, a breath.

être vieux,
assis sur le bout de bois de dieu,
je vois plus loin que claire et liam…

to see beyond what youth can yet imagine is to hold the long view. it's a call to live with intention, to live fully in the present while honoring the past.

so when you reach the final poem and read:
you can breathe

know that this is not the end.
it's the beginning of something else—
something tender, hard-won, and deeply human.

you can breathe.
you are breathing.
you are becoming.

ylva isabelle blondel
saturday, 4 october 2025
stockholm, sweden

acknowledgments

this collection began in san miguel de allende, a global creative hub. my first steps into the 20th writer's conference were guided by jailan adley. judyth hill, whose workshop, "writing through grief: bringing our broken-open heart to the page," gave me the inspiration to reimagine my writing. to explore the layers of grief, i listened deeply to the people who believed in the light shining within me.

i am who i am because of the hymns and psalms that nursed my premature life. I owe so much to the silent prayers of my late maternal grandmother and grandfather, and to my late father and mother, who taught me patience in the darkest hours.

i am indebted to claire and liam, who taught me about the journey to fatherhood by allowing me to witness their destinies. their presence is a testament to the belief that dreams from abidjan and belleville could meet to form one family with lelani.

my writing is better because of the aspen new voices fellowship and the invaluable guidance of emily kaiser, andrew quinn, rachael strecher, and holly kearl. They polished my words and refined my voice to resonate with editors and readers across the world.

no work is complete without judyth hill's and mary meade's guiding hands, astute minds, and eyes for the finer details. mary and judyth of wild rising press, medaase.

may each word in this collection find a string in your heart, so that we may all embrace grief on the path to prosperity.

author's biography

carl manlan is an emerging voice in
contemporary poetry. his writing
navigates the holistic landscape
of human emotion and explores
the delicate balance between loss
and renewal, often finding beauty
in the most challenging of human

experiences. a native of Abidjan, Côte d'Ivoire, his creative
work is a reflection of his own life experiences, particularly the
profound shifts that follow loss. with a background in policy,
finance, and social impact, he brings a raw and empathetic lens
to his poetry. *i can breathe* is his debut collection, born from
a deeply personal journey through grief and a quiet search
for inner light; it is a poignant and hopeful exploration of
how prosperity blooms from the ashes of grief. when he is
not writing, carl enjoys learning from his children, his source
of *bien être*, well-being. he invites readers to connect with
him online at carlmanlanofficial.com, @carlmanlanofficial on
instagram & tiktok, as well as @carlmanlan on linkedin.

this book's titles are set in andale mono and the body text in bell mt, two faces in quiet conversation—each carrying its own history of clarity and grace, one modern, one ancient. andale mono, designed in 1993 by steven r. matteson, is a "monospaced type," every letter holding equal space. every character stands evenly apart, like a steady, deliberate breath, opening each poem with calm, steadfast rhythm—the measured pulse of healing. this clean, unornamented font telegraphs the poems' devotion to truth—the clean incision of language seeking to set the broken right, and the calm authority of the poet's voice that carries through the book. bell mt, developed in 1788, the heart of the age of enlightenment, by the punchcutter richard austin for the british letter foundry run by visionary publisher, john bell, reflects the deeply humanist values of its time—harmony, serenity, and balance. bell's tender curves pair warmth with the cool precision of andale mono, as in this collection, intellect is suffused with compassion, as love outlasts loss. formal, classical, bell mt conveys a deep sense of gravitas. like the poems in *i can breathe*, its refined strokes and serif detailing exude tremendous dignity and a sense of standing in literary tradition. bell mt is controlled, balanced, as if the poet's "silence long kept loud inside" has been gently exhaled onto the page, with unique character and tremendous personal integrity. these two fonts, joined across time on these pages, hold this legacy of care and clarity, a testament to two fathers' enduring wisdom and goodness, a grief luminous with gratitude, an offering of beauty and courage.

www.ingramcontent.com/pod-product-compliance
Lightning Source LLC
Chambersburg PA
CBHW071754120626
46550CB00002B/783